Hand
Me
the
Limits

Hand Me the Limits

Ted Rees

ROOF BOOKS
New York

ISBN: 979-8-9896652-2-8

Library of Congress Control Number: 2024932590

Edited by Lonely Christopher
Cover and interior design by Kate Robinson
Cover photo by Theodore Jung
Author photo by the author

NEW YORK STATE OF OPPORTUNITY. | Council on the Arts   This book is made possible by the New York State Council on the Arts with the support of Governor Kathy Hochul and the New York State Legislature

Roof Books
are published by
Segue Foundation
300 Bowery, New York, NY 10012
seguefoundation.com

Roof Books
are distributed by
Small Press Distribution
1341 Seventh Street
Berkeley, CA 94710-1403
800-869-7553 or spdbooks.org

Table of Contents

Prologue:
"Everything Becomes Rearranged"

Everything becomes rearranged
words like "stage" and some numerals
are immovable traps when the hum
is your weathered companion

beeping machines elevators small and large whooshes of
fluid droplets car tires losing air organ being restored
pounding of magnetic imaging cylinders turning inside and
next to each other around your hips chest shaved remnants
floating in tub heat of laser smooth along crown fingers
slipping through pages and pages of books fans blowing
idiotically blowing him and loosing poison on sheets
a tendency in your elbow a way of keeping it down in
shower mask pumping over face we don't stop
'til the screaming starts
you dig
the hum

That's the hum

lips at the end of a paper towel roll softly blowing
in your ear each moment
we begin and end in holes
complexities of the mother's arrival

Convalesce in scenes from the thorax
calmly debating the purpose
of its own empire
there on the slab
curing for weeks
ribs expand as you position
a string in your mind
connecting the dots in the ceiling

with the tat above your dick
leaking urethra song
about rainbows elsewhere
lachrymose parking lot

Your neck stiffened
phone greasy at ear
he keeps asking you questions
closing your eyes you see
his fire escape hair
slicked back and sudden rise
in register, hand on your ass
kiss or something like it

kiss out of you out of my
interruption in services

A remembrance for your new void
less shallow perhaps
than the one you describe here
subject lethargic and confused
and wanting to be filled
a proper tube again and
again told to jump higher
gravel unfolding in teeth
unable to really suss
the remaining unsevered nerve complex
ain't that a shame
if you can't dance, too

Make Me Real, Make Me Sick

The evening after they discovered the tumor growing inside of me, I found myself sitting in my small home office, completing the last bits of the semester's grading. Seemingly out of the ether, the lyrics of a song came to me: *And I know it, I can't see it / But I know it enough to believe it.* I put my pen down, rested my head against the window next to my desk, and closed my eyes. From where did Hole's "Jennifer's Body" arrive? Why this song, now? My thoughts were plangent, and as the melody and lyrics continued to run through me, I was transported to the smazy memory of my younger self staring out a car window at a yellowing beach town, mouthing the words, "Sleeping with my enemy myself."

⁂

It was in the spring of 1995 that my mother was diagnosed with stage IV invasive epithelial ovarian cancer, and it was late in the summer of that year that I was taken on vacation by my friend D's parents. I don't remember much about the vacation itself—a snapshot of bodysurfing, a faint recollection of falling asleep at a late-night screening of *Waterworld*—but I do recall the car ride from Philadelphia, particularly the music piping through my cheap headphones: Hole's *Live Through This*, Rancid's *Let's Go!*, a sample CD from the *College Music Journal* featuring songs by Teenage Fanclub and the Circle Jerks that fascinated me. The interstate became clogged and dusty, two-lane, and as I sat in my office, I could recall the intermittent view of a wave rolling toward shore interrupted by rows of stilted clapboard vacation homes, all while Courtney Love wailed, "Make me real, fuck you."

It was a rasping demand that I appreciated back then. My mother spent most of her time in bed or on the couch, gray and vomiting and suddenly hyper-religious, while my father worked in the day and spent sleepless nights caring for her. His parents lived with us for a while. Besides games of Scrabble and gin rummy, we all found few ways to bridge the gaps between us. I had friends, of course, and their well-meaning parents who carted us around to various activities or allowed us free reign to run around, but none of it mattered to me. It all seemed like a prefab distraction to which I was supposed to resign myself. Because I couldn't shake the feeling that it was a well-meaning ruse, I also couldn't slough the inkling that there was something deeply wrong with me, that I was an unreal target of an immense plot.

In my head, the vacation with D and his family remains at the center of this plot, of this whole time period, even though many specifics of the sojourn near the seaside have slipped away. Other than the music that obsessed me, my sharpest memory of the trip is when, during the last slog in the family sedan, I proclaimed that Courtney Love was a genius. For a moment, D's mom and dad looked at each other. Then one of them dismissed my enthusiasm by denigrating Love as "crazy" or something similarly pejorative.

The contemptuous tone of their reaction solidified what had already been congealing: that my dim view of my circumstances as a being in this world would never be recognized as legitimate, and that the conspiracy of distraction was not imagined. I was not presumed by adults or anyone else to feel anger, pain, or bitterness, and when the extraordinarily vivid reality of those emotions came to the fore, they could be discarded by others as easily as my expressions of joy and exuberance, of identification. I put my headphones back on: *No one cares, my friends*.

❧

I've never been able to accurately describe the feelings that I felt then. Even now I find the depiction above inadequate to a degree matched only by the poor consolation that had been offered. It made me gasp, then, when I was reading through the recent "shorter" edition of *The Norton Anthology of Short Fiction* during class prep and came across Alice Munro's story, "Miles City, Montana." Within the first two pages, a local boy dies tragically, and the child narrator finds herself looking at the adults at the boy's funeral with "a furious and sickening disgust . . . [that] had nothing sharp and self-respecting about it . . . It could not be understood or expressed, though it died down after a while into a heaviness, then just a taste, an occasional taste—a thin, familiar misgiving." What Munro's narrator discerns in herself is a bile and rage marked by an obliquity of reason, yes, but it is not entirely directionless—the adults are culpable in *some nefarious act*, and they seem undoubtedly deserving of the narrator's scorn. But the specifics of that act, however familiar it might be, remain mysterious.

After reading this first section of Munro's story, I let the weighty book fall from my hands, onto my chest. What was this intimate act that so troubled her narrator, that so disturbed my own sense of well-being as a child? How did her narrator manage to respond to this ignorance of the source of her own anger? How did she survive? How did I?

In an entry included in the introduction to *The Cancer Journals*, Audre Lorde writes that there is "no device to separate [her] struggle within from [her] fury at the outside world's viciousness, the stupid brutal lack of consciousness or concern that passes for the way things are." This illuminates part of what is happening to Munro's narrator, and what was happening to me in 1995, albeit under very different circumstances. The inextricability of which Lorde writes is matched by, and might be constitutive of, the "heaviness" that Munro's narrator feels. That this feeling can lead down many labyrinthine paths wracked by suffering is a given. How these paths fascinate and sustain, though, is what should most interest the living.

Thus, for me, punk rock was never about skateboarding or a modish hewing to outlandish fashion choices. It was about a firm belief that there was a senselessness to what caused both the familiar—the "struggle within"—and the ever-shifting machinations of the world around me. My own furies, confusions, and happinesses were rendered immaterial and unreal by the people with whom I interacted, and those same people seemed petty and oblivious regarding the brutalities punctuating the world beyond their doorsteps. No wonder I felt like an alien, and no wonder Love's exhortations—"Make me real, come on," with a pronounced increase in throatiness on the three final syllables—initiated me into a realm where demanding the impossible was viewed as perfectly reasonable.

In returning to "Miles City, Montana," Munro's narrator, now an adult, recollects her younger self viewing her parents at the neighborhood boy's funeral:

> I was understanding that they were implicated... They gave consent to the death of children and to my death not by anything they said or thought but by the very fact that they had made children... even then I knew they were not to blame. But I did blame them.

It would be easy to say that Munro's narrator was in rebellion against death, but really, she was in rebellion against "effrontery, hypocrisy," against the snares of "vanquished grownups, with their sex and funerals." Like punk rock, it is an impossible rebellion, but one with a sincerity of feeling, veritably drenched in empathy—righteous and perfect in its righteousness. It raises its fist against the "stupid brutal lack of consciousness" that Lorde decries, and which made me so miserable as a child. I wanted honesty, and what I got were adults trying to shield my eyes from nurses plunging needles filled with poison into my mother's flesh, adults attempting to find new routes so as to not to expose me to the collapsing, abandoned houses in mostly Black neighborhoods stretching for miles in our home city, adults steering me away from the profane and defiant because they were frightened of the real and wanted to pass that self-preserving fear on to me. And because I wasn't having what Born Against's Sam McPheeters calls the "smiling commodity that isn't human," I can still see myself alone in my room at age eleven, alone in my room at age thirteen, alone in my room at age fourteen, whirling around and mouthing lyrics to shambolic, naive, pissed-off songs that won't ever get old or die.

&

A little more than a week ago, on my first day of chemotherapy, I found myself alone in my infusion suite, a bit of a throb emanating from the IV in my right arm. In my left hand was a copy of *Light Sweet Crude*, a book of collaborative poems and lyrics by Vancouver poets Nancy Shaw and Catriona Strang. I'd become slightly obsessed with Shaw's work during a trip to Vancouver last fall and had received the book as a Christmas gift right after my tumor had been biopsied and diagnosed. That Shaw had passed away from cancer in the middle of her collaboration with Strang was a fact not lost on me when I unwrapped the book on Christmas Eve, nor was it lost on me in the antiseptic yet cocoon-like warmth of the suite where life-saving poison dripped into my arm.

Yet again I gasped, for as I approached the book's end, I noticed liberal quotes from Courtney Love's lyrics to "Violet" and "Olympia" smattered throughout the text much as they are smattered in this essay. The songs, which had meant so much to me as a child and which had been reverberating in my head since the day following the discovery of my tumor, proved a perfectly sly inclusion in a group of poems determined to interrogate and engage with the sublime, "its envelopment of the beauty and/or horror of the self, nature, war, kindness, passion, and disaster." Like Strang and Shaw's work, Love's lyrics embrace contradiction, particularly with regard to visions of the self, putting the lie to the myth of the unified subject. The book, which had been pretty wonderful in the minutes before, became exciting, and then it became something else.

It was when I reached "www.sorry.com," a late poem in Strang and Shaw's "Cold Trip" sequence, that I began to weep, to wrap my head around my more pressing and present mortality. Here it is:

> My sincere apology
> I repeat, I was
> Roving very fast
> Set my pulse
> To obsolesce
>
> I'm the one with no soul
> I told you from the start
> How this will end
> I lament my fate
> As sentimental hate
>
> Love stops innocence
> Journey and curve
> The apology, you answer
> I cannot talk more than usual
> When clouds deny twilight
> To close the distance
> Measured in lies
>
> Despite the times
> I will illuminate
> Weeks of withering
> Witnessed in every single line
> We look the same

We talk the same
My dear supporters

The purchaser sells the sky
Is this progress
You know it's all
Squandered
As a consequence
You brighten up
That I thought
You would flatter me

The poem astounded me and continues to do so. It begins with an apology, appropriate since an expression of regret is usually the first phrase that leaves peoples' lips when confronted with illness. Strangely, the apology is often mirrored by the sufferer and becomes part of a recursive phrasal economy of mutual sympathy—an infinitude of "I'm sorry"s resounding through all interaction. My partner, my mother, my father, my friend, even total strangers are all sorry, and I am sorry that they are sorry, and it pains me that we are so filled with sorrow because of this growth that is inside of me that none of us could have predicted. I would that our sorrow could be channeled elsewhere.

The poem then moves quickly through implications of fast living and planned obsolescence to Gins-like rejoinders against the reaper, arriving at the first insertion of Love's lyrics. Here we are confronted by the afflicted person's acquiescence to the societal demand that the sick individual has "no soul" and only sickness, a demand that is particularly onerous when mortality is part of the equation—even if the afflicted individual knows "how this will end," society craves the sick person as an emblem of noble suffering, soulless as the person might be. Many who are placed in the position of the ill patient lament this treatment, as it makes manifest a contradiction—the suffering person is both monumentalized and despised. That so many cancer patients see a few good friendships drop off after their diagnosis is certainly evidence of this latter characteristic that defines even intimate views of the afflicted body.

We are then granted a return to the apology, its recursion becoming more evident, but here made slant by love (or Love?) and its habit of forcing culpability onto the afflicted subject and sympathizers alike. What is this guilt? I read Strang and Shaw's words as suggesting that it results from the haziness of the distance toward death—"clouds deny twilight"—but there is also the closeness of that distance, particularly for Shaw, and it is "measured in lies" that deny that closeness as a result of love. The afflicted does not want to quit love, and neither do her sympathizers, and so both resort to lies to keep the body wrapped (and rapt) in the intransigent yet intimate bonds of love that can only be found in platonic friendship. What my younger self desired was exactly what Strang and Shaw seem to be doing here: acknowledging the lies that abound in the relations between those who are ill and their families, friends, and associates. The acknowledgment doesn't diminish any feelings of tenderness and affection; instead, it serves as a method of viewing the distance between the now of illness and the far (or near) place of mortality.

And then there are the lines of Shaw and Strang's poem that most buoyed me, these lines that forge a determination and a continuing: "Despite the times / I will illuminate / Weeks of withering / Witnessed in every single line." It is difficult to have cancer, yes, but it is also difficult to have one's cancer constantly framed in bellicose terms, especially when one is not a bellicose person. Thus, that the lines frame the "witnessed" documentation of "withering" as part of a process of illumination gives solace, because while I remain that furious alien teenager in many ways, my diagnosis finds me more interested in illuminating as a form of yelling. Love arrives again, too, and becomes part of the admonishment not just to "dear supporters," but also to the wider world, transforming Love's alienation into a unifying rally, "We look the same / We talk the same." There is, too, the suggestion that in the end, we are these fleshy husks, that there is a flattening of difference that comes when our bodies turn cold.

I can't imagine a poem closer to my complex of feelings as I sat in that curtained-off zone, the crackle of TV babble from other patients nearby, the smell of Chinese takeout wafting the floor's corridors. I realized that part of why I'd wept while reading it for the first time was not only the synchronicity of its message with my surroundings and the linkages of cancer and illness strung between me with Shaw, but also the rage that I share with both poets. It is not an easy anger, but it arrives from empathic nodes, from that space that does not want to be sick because the world is sick enough, and there is forever the compulsion and need to challenge such sickness. As I'd walked into the medical building that morning, I'd passed by a homeless man begging for change, coughing something terrible. Though my privilege has allowed me the modicum of comfort that shitty insurance provides, the conditions that create his sickness are the same that create mine, and neither of us should have to shoulder the burden of this agony.

But my body suffers, the bodies of so many others suffer, and I only have so many methods of placing blame for that suffering, for the "squandered" world I inhabit for now. One of those is crying and another is crying out, and so I will do both heedlessly into the indeterminacy of the months ahead.

1/24/19

Hand Me the Limits

I want things
to be things
I didn't know
before I turned them
to storm
                    —Clark Coolidge, *"Below as Beyond"*

What primal kinetics
schmeared th'occasion
but the rank fever
that is the fear
of venom, uncertain
species at any hour
or to say, we praise
the box you've made,
vague tint in your eyes
a sort of unspeakable
violence or corner
of a room, greasy
dust a glue that's hard
to get off.

Soup were the option
and thus we folded
into these drifts, certainly
playing cassino, yodeling
into the trash that filmed
and films my sight,
the faint barber of time
clipping you into shapes
swept into crackle, dry
ribbon my fist followed
through to my nudity
in mirror, drug me
despising the beads'
whisper in your dull head
and southern exposure
deleting every day,
never more wanting
to be wetter.

Shimmied up the fallen
snag aloft at rest
where I plotted
my abandonment
of my plectrum,
wasted on wrong
lessons like the rooster
at your insistence
dissing the blood
around my skull
or the fey rhythm
my boyish tits bounce
to, prodded by poor
circulation in fingers
or it's the dent
that cannot be sucked.

Shoesies pinching in the lot's
long path to narthex, a slur
you threw at me, put out
of my mind righteous
fresh scab each hour
three decades after,
I cannot help but arrange
hurt and quit myself then
in wound, I recognize
how these mean gurgles
swap in and out but
their front resents
their asses, you understand
how language inheres
or doesn't, tell me more.

Held unlit 'tween
teeth, baby fluffing
over in all flesh big
baby boy, your mama
in the mind's pew, big
fluff more like my own
heat merely touching
stomach in the cold,
where I descended
unrecalled but around
this time, puffing in
the woods next
the tracks, eyes on
each syllable his lips
formed and so, high
as high goes like
chasing is natural
or never to return.

Rent as I could
or on my knees
with my legs tucked
"breaking the law"
in the magazines,
we did, we'd a heap
of hours shirking
each other out of
existence, pale
you misunderstood
the pale boy's pout
and I never forgave
you, your healing,
your only dread
my fingers limning
his, with certainty
he closed me, cool
milk his face poured
onto my shoulder,
and pours like this
poem I've written
before never mentioned
the movie we saw:
Tomorrow Never Dies,
the distance between
insanity and genius
or something less
more likely.

I swallowed melody
as purpose, my knees
in the grass you are
so fond of, flailing
skeletally in want

as though mimicry
could rally the sense
of myself for you,
elsewhere my Schwinn
and moustache wisps
circling the access
road to the tracks,
that is, relieved
of duty inasmuch
as I owe you
a pinch of nested
tumult and fear,
or another name
for the vein show.

It never occurred
to me to drool
as testimony but bottom
lip it beads, refracting
the limbs that forget
except feet shuffling
and the air feast
said to be song,
to be a drill
for how to shake off
how long a stretch
maybe remains.

Rendered as clean
for those months, inaccurate
spilling the bells you'd call
pretty or try to rake
into the suplex denying
all my claims, my skin
on the mat, a hint
like a cake you forgot
where to look, so sad
the chords I whistled,
that is the root and that
is my sweat there
upper lip quivering

We basic pose
smoking in the kitchen,
evading the melt
our illusions burden themselves
with until puddled, the very image
of health at rest there
at our feet, not as clear
as I'd like, so we live
through tubes we maneuver
pumping to the terminal
and rearranged tubes,
emergent holes like years
washed like little tubes
down the throat, impervious
to language even now:
the click of all that brightness
that you remember also,
grace of touching what comes
after without being pulled
in, still wanting out and out,
my hands and hooves
tingling in the flesh I inform
about an extended warranty.

It is beaten and then
some so you lick it
and defend its sugar
industry, the unweathered
that is your weeping
cynic's affinity for lining
inflatable heart pasture,
deface me some more
because I so enjoy resting
my scowl at the top
of your spine.

Ill and jammed into,
you saw the water
dripping at pace
from my wrists tho,
silver pouch or not.

Hasten to fold
though I decide late
to spread, saunter
like a Shetland pony
revelation, or how
I've formed my vase
as container, worse,
nutriment for the that
what bathes your lips.

Making the case
poorly with loads
of hooey, try again
to genetic cancer.
Easy to say, I could
not breathe at infusion
so I stayed in pink
limbo for another hour,
the true knife of it
a dangling or swing
at throat, I fell in
to my skin's aluminum
ennui and crumpled.

Oy, oy, bleak fancy
always losing juice
on the grill or never
without a disarming
smile, turbid and maybe
righteous arrival
from your day drink,
the summer commands
in its wretched glopping
shriek the sort of grief
you love like not
believing it's not,
you never lined around
the feed for government
cheese and it shows.

The Failures of Fellowship

Or if if sometimes if
—Laura Riding, *"All the Time"*

Type of project: writing/sculpture/performance

Project Description: I would like to utilize the ████████ fellowship to think around questions of complicity, culpability, metaphor, pain, and illness through the lens of someone currently undergoing treatment for cancer. How is the cancer-stricken body viewed, and how is it performed? How do metaphors of illness in literature and other contemporary media both diminish and monumentalize the cancerous body? How does care enact itself? Does the toxic battling the toxic extend to the way in which humans interact with the Anthropocene era? What role does the patient's pain have in a world that already demands pain of most of its inhabitants? What are the afterlives of both organic and inorganic medical waste? Where does it hurt and why?

I will attempt to search through these questions by using my own experiences in the medical-industrial complex as starting points. For example, while spending inordinate amounts of time in waiting rooms, occasionally with loved ones, I've wondered how these spaces blasting HGTV and filled with celebrity magazines are constitutive of both the causes of the illness and comforts then offered the cancer patient. In addition, while undergoing MRIs and radiation therapy, I've pondered the aural and technological connections between medical machinery and experimental music practices evident in works such as Yasunao Tone's *Solo for Wounded CD* and Holly Herndon's *Proto*. Finally, it is also impossible not to notice that the number of medications that I must take is unwieldy, grotesque, and sickening, and so is the amount of plastic that is utilized and then discarded throughout the average sick person's journey. Perhaps most symbolic of this latter symptom of late capital are the ubiquitous amber pill bottles utilized by most pharmacies.

I plan on using the platform of ███████ as a method of sharing progress leading up to a cumulative event—a dynamic and interactive performance wherein I will create a sculpture of approximately 250 amber pill bottles stuffed with excerpts from my writings accumulated and published by ███████ during the fellowship. Over the course of the event, I will share these writings with an audience through movement and speech, combining Antin-like improvisations and more prescriptive text and embodiment. In addition, audience members will at certain points be encouraged to engage with the pill bottles and share their contents.

My contributions to ███████ during the lead-up to the performance event will include reviews of related literature selections (Johanna Hedva's *Sick Woman Theory*, Mary F.E. Ebeling's *Healthcare and Big Data: Digital Spectres and Phantom Objects*, and Karen Brodine's work among these), thoughts on current media environments contained in hospitals, blog posts on music's therapeutic effects during times of immense bodily stress and pain, a potential interview with Anne Boyer, as well as videos of constructing the sculpture to be utilized in the cumulative performance.

While primarily a poetry performance project, I'm also interested in the idea of the pill bottles as forming a kind of book or library of my particular experience with cancer, and could easily see an e-publication arising out of the project as well.

Big Dearth in Whir

My dainties griefe shall be, and teares my poisned wine
—John Coprario, *Funeral Teares (IIII.7)*

Criable shoreline
a harness like a bad merge,
gritty tongue lesson
cracking the spine
post sexing.

All bells depend
on their plunge,
I'm there bless me,

bless my gowns

dummy naked mind
bayou.

I stood slowly
draped in pain
pills and oils
berating like
a mimic or world,

I felt the big belly
reclined in yurt
unswept and haloed
surrendering as
this tone in my song,

I rinsed my mouth
fastened in grit
nostalgic ochre
doormat to
some prehistoric
exceptions wriggling my gullet.

Correct as quoted
at numerous desks
I kept swallowing
and lost in the reeds

Imagine absorbing
all that sun into
your shell, where
I laugh from as in
I worshipped there once
and slick told me
of our perfection,
yearn for paper skin
and an instinct or two.

My first names'
echolocation shimmer
there, a sort of stew
tight on linoleum.

We pressed in
as a daydream
flew fancy down
the sides, yours
mingling with toxins
sporting sunglasses
eruptive and bright,
a good curse.

We made the river
I thought we made
knees grind glass
I love this lament
you in it, too.

The draft in melody
we took as rictus
or summer ransom,
tepid shower don
the loose cotton
where I approach
festering by the door
I rappel down my center
each second a regret.

Tallowed therefore
face underwater

rubbing my crevice
with sentences
as thin as I am
disloyal to these
dunes' present
crackle, not at all,
zilch as formal
distillate despite
a run on parts.

Our peninsulas
where we wake
cinch more then more,
light's hung and I
leaned into this
spine we fused
or are fusing
for a new release
in the next decade,
freaky but Dougies
just like I like it.

Petted as valid
surprise hairless,
fed me blast site
when the storm
was always already,

meaning despicable.
Interrogatives abound
but you can't see
and there my stream
goes, toodles.

Came out slithering
post creation myth

jealous of the expanse
rather opposed to
the tiny pit
of my weeks

rude, that failure
that is the probe
lubed, my tapping
on farthest screen
from want and wrong
noun, forgive me
cruelly, as we've come
to expect.

Blasted forage
for the right welt,

some transcripts
diminished conversants
desire excised, I felt

some angle of my prism
dreary in dirndl slip
away and into wooden

gourds to not eat
but shake and admire
their resonance.

Collapsed into divan
as long as the silk
moth flutters in
scattered switchbacks.

Abandon your camp,
this brings good fortune.
I spoke funny, and you
spoke funny, too,
inert in our tonguing
the next five years.

He blinks blandly,
sage and untethered
a vapor in the rows
like a babble one's forgot,
the culture of the child
screaming for gratis
wrapped graham cracker,
wet deli slice microwaved.

Beyond what brews
at the airport, salty
and reflective massif
with bottle 'n' spuds.

My fingers on your spot,
where I remember it being.

Twang an ideal
through the window's fine
dust layer, wind in
my hole, my boudoir
pollinated and blood
on the folding table's
hacked stolidity.

If it sounds naked,
think about it fessing
up to you, your jokes
in your puffed cheeks
about the rearranged
indoors situation.

Share that place
in your thighs with crowds
or the soiled magazines
will wend their memories
to you a decade on,
they wait in the drive-thru
looking rumpled with saliva
round their mugs, cold
snap and I can't feel again.

Whet mine,
rip off a hunk
then come,
aim at me.
It repeats how
it yells, you catch?
a hum that stirs
the gut or guts,
clear tone pain
per usual, laundry
day tomorrow

Rather escarole
wilting in the hoop
target como skin
on skin dynamited.

Monday and
the river rolls
your socks on my mind
sheets
you turned me around
then the shutter.

That such a shade
called Fresh Lawn
were nimble in my inferno
baked in cream genre
limitations we sour
on like press-on
floors, big dearth
in whir my pelvis
nicely framed

Likewise I
pinning the yolk
hushed, slipped
deranged babbling
deeper in
my banter.

Keep putting on
the same accent
to sing each morning.

Until Dallas or grease fire
decline okay splendid
playing a corpse
in the field as the swells
build their slush
in very Kelly
and wet slate
rushing toward the falls
down straightaway,
worst time of day
for these visions
the irradiated viscera
challenge feebly,
remember otherwise
adjusting to the dew
bending off my arm.

Dotted pronunciation
cling for a day
to where my sex
might wander,
its nightly poison
resonant chew.

When swallowed
the fur line continues
to be hackled

so said dismal
punching the button
clench, shining
sticker applies

harangue of pity,
its brutish texture
speeding the spring
from structure as
likely, leafy

inspecting the bottoms
of my shoes.

Tardy is the word
most vivid in marbles
but it was all over,
I went skipping
into the piercing
forcefed
forcefed

we laid about
festive meats
branded at undercarriage,
proper tunnel
like we needed
a good choke,
Kokomo in my thoughts.

There is canned
and canned again
true to scythe, cold
as Duluth might be,
hacking continuance.

My shredded bits
of paper I am
the hyper dread
lost in the bark
clucking furious.

I saddled myself
you can and cannot
see my foliage
mine and electric
impossible the eyelids.

Right as haste
becomes murmur
at the takeout:

bye-bye droplets
and rattling jars
stuffed with my beef
smeared in Concord.

I wanted that bumper,
that window, I wanted
evasive maneuvers,
my back rubbing the trunk
and so far shadowed
that you squint
into the bark and stare.

At the stake
but us all
malodorous
drab at the watch
infer our march

place our fingers
abandoning our wounds

our hardwood floors
glisten, and that's
good in the commute
to the trap
we approach daily,
nude and shined
heading out
as heading in.

The idea a dog
running, hymn
in yelp and pant,
maybe lips' initials
becoming when pressed.

Like what of scrapes
the needs of the vise
of halls, jagged at back
of mouth, coiled
in sleep and the still

that I so want to adapt
to my veins, you squeeze
my battery and we rifle
the plum side this evening
all the way home.

Dear Kevin

Dear Kevin,

Seven days after your physical body left us, Theo and I sat down to watch *Un couteau dans le coeur*, the 2018 film about a murderer killing a gay porn studio's models in late 1970's Paris. I'd been watching Argento and Bava films while re-reading your *Argento Series*, and the reviews made *Un couteau* seem like it might be a successor to *gialli*, plus it was queer and starred some gorgeous actors, so win-win, right? I thought it might cheer me some, since your absence had been palpable all week, my spirit bereft.

The film transported me back to the period when we first became close, when I was your student and you my mentor. At the time, I spent most of my hours outside of reading and writing on a search for other young men to sleep with. I wrote about San Francisco and my dreams, about web-cam videos and capitalism, about the itinerant life I found myself dwelling within, and you pushed and encouraged me always. You saw something in me that I had trouble seeing inside of myself, really, as I hopped from bed to bed. We crushed on each other, but our affection was based in intellectual and social affinities, mostly. It continued this way for years, even after I moved away. You made me feel worthwhile and loved unlike any other person I've known.

The film ended with the murder victims and their loved ones alive, caressing and smiling at each other in a room resplendent with white. Your lover Arthur Russell once sang, "I wanna see all my friends at once," and the finale seemed in that spirit. I wept then laughed, thinking of you now in a similar room with so many of your friends, how lucky they are and how lucky we were to have been with you here on Earth.

Love always,
Ted

Can't Get You Out of My Head

Don't be frightened
Just give me a little bit more
            —Kylie Minogue, *"All the Lovers"*

Love always,
I never let this happen.

I do not feel sorry for anyone but
myself. I had always dreamed
I would be the first
person to become a true
love, but never, ever again,
I thought I would be the first
man to come
out of the world,

I thought I would be the first
human being.

I was so lucky in this life
that I loved to
have my own voice
in my mind.

Like crinkled aluminum foil,
a piece of paper, or piece of plastic.

A piece of paper with a hole in
it. A piece of paper with a
hole in it.
A piece of paper with a hole in it. A piece of paper with
a hole in it.

The wall in front of a wall,
and I couldn't get the doors open.

But I knew I had to make it open, the way
the whole place is.
I felt

the way a stone has to be made to open a wall.
That is what I wanted to do.
And I didn't know how.

- appetite loss
- gastrointestinal problems, including upset stomach and constipation
- fatigue
- weakness
- headaches
- changes in taste
- hair loss
- abdominal aches
- methroidism
- sugar
- unions
- shorts
- eating in a bowl of water
- eating a steak
- eating a banana
- eating a pizza
- eating a carrot
- eating a steak
- eating a banana
- eating
- a chicken
- eating a fruitcake
- eating a banana
- eating a chicken
- eating a cucumber
- eating a strawberry
- eating a tomato
- eating a strawberry
- eating a tomato
- eating a strawberry
- eating a fruitcake
- eating a strawberry
- eating a strawberry
- eating a strawberry

Came after me.
You can't see my lips
like my eyes
so slightly dark and light
so it looks like I've got the
wish of the
sun

so I'm sure my lips
like my hands
so I'm sure my lips
like my hands
chapped deranged
dropping skin

so I was trying to
be in an

I could see the
wish of
the
wish of the sun

so I'm sure my lips
like my hands
could eat or attempt
to eat the dance
of you

I can't
just imagine

you're just waiting for
me to say more

but bone ache
my stupid disposition
are not my
yet
I can't do it anymore

"I really love the idea of that," he said.

"I know it's a dream I have in my heart to make.

"I want to make it something that's not just a dream, it's a dream I've dreamed.

"I can't get it back from the world of a dream, I'm just not going to.

"I need to make something that's not just a dream. It's a dream I've dreamed of.

"I want to be happy. I want to be happy.

"I can't get back from the world of a dream, I'm just not going to."

"They just stopped.

"We went out and I could see
how the air was running.

"It was just like we had to do that
on that plane," he said.

"It wasn't the plane," I said.

There was nothing.

It was the air we would put up,
or anything else we would do,
and the whole thing
was completely controlled.

"It was just a piece of paper,"
he said.

"I remember sitting on that plane
at the end of the night," he said.

"That's it," I said.

"What do you think? What is it
going to look like, man?"

I was like, wow.

"It's like a piece of paper,"
I said, he nodded

and said, "It's just this, it's
this...

I can't wait to see."

I didn't think we had a story
to tell, but I guess

I didn't know anything.

I can sense it: I donk

in the backyard—
when I saw one day
and just walked inside of it
with a bottle, with only my hand
still still tied
between each strand.

As a toddler, to watch my body melt
as if in its deep-pocketed embrace
while living and dead and for every
single goddamn damn damn hole
to dig to hole without my mind
ever waking back down that same
little white plastic ball,

you've always known
the little creature I didn't even want
that could actually exist.

And so I'll come here
and say to the world,
"that you'll be a little happy."

That's not the way to go,
but I'll have to wait for you.

"For the rest of the day
you will not be alone."

You'll find yourself waiting
for the day, and it is no longer
just me,

"But my way of being
not alone is to be proud."

What can go beyond the pain
of sitting outside without looking
beyond its bounds, no matter
what is not right, it's funny

when I see them who look
young, sucking from a man
of 20 and a pair of earpins,

a thin blue earnut crown perched
at the window of my bedroom
that has alluring resemblance
to that other man with little inimitable hair.

At last the song broke my spirit.

The only way I understand I must have just realized what it felt... to go to an empty room next door... to stay in that darkness, I took some small, non-physical lessons away from a large window just a week prior in the fall from school after an hour at the same point that they found a body

Taking Revenge on the World
for Not Existing

I.

A few years ago, I was mentioned in a conversation between Brandon and Thom that was published in *BOMB* magazine's online repository. For a while, it was one of the top results when you Googled my name, so that any person who might have wanted to know something about me and clicked on the right sequence of links got Brandon saying, "I love Ted. He's so fucking punk. You know?"

Let me tell you: that really pissed me off. Being recognized is terrible. It is having a fucked mirror placed to your body that reflects only the most outlandish identifiers. But the fact is that for years following the publication of my dear friends' back-and-forth, I remained in full embrace of punk's signifiers, or at least some variation thereof: I bleached my hair or had total hack job haircuts. I rode freight trains. I lived and fucked in punk houses and squats filled with trash and drugs and no electricity. I wore ridiculously shambling clothes often haphazardly sewn together with dental floss.

I wallowed in punk, rolled around in its effluvia, rambled through its alleys strewn with rigs and snipes and glass shards and screeching speeding sweat. And all the while, I was also writing poetry and giving talks about gentrification and Wojnarowicz and reading Dodie and Kevin and Dennis and Megan Camille and Bob and Bruce, and relatedly, Bataille.

Admittedly, I now find this period of my life or "development" utterly embarrassing, one of the ugliest of the ugly feelings. But from where my discomfort arrives, I am not certain. Sometimes, I think it comes from years of investment in a community of affect that has little to do with what I now hold dear in this world. At other times, I am chagrinned by punk's avowed distrust of and antipathy toward any sort of nuance. Yet simultaneously, the DIY punk ethos and its relation to an undermining of capitalist hegemony seems embedded within my spirit, continuing to wend its way through what I write and how I teach and the thoughts with which I spend my time on a quotidian basis. A short-lived anarchist punk band once wrote in a communique, "punk is a ghetto," and I tend to agree with the declaration, but extricating oneself from that cultural slum, especially as a queer person, is not simple, particularly if one has spent a good portion of one's life inside of it.

II.

In a 1997 *College Music Journal* review of *I Am That Great And Fiery Force*, the first full-length record by queercore band Behead the Prophet No Lord Shall Live, poet Stephanie Burt writes,

> Behead [...] plays top-speed, slightly sloppy, cheaply recorded, metal-inflected hardcore punk, with tangled-up rapid-fire bass-guitar showmanship, drums like a hailstorm on a car crash in an avalanche, and high-pitched screaming about authority and oppression.

Especially for a pop critic, Burt gets the sound right, but the missing element from the review is mention of the music's confrontational, violent queerness. Vocalist Joshua Ploeg's shredded throatings are deliriously scrambled and ambiguously pitched so that they are outside of gender; thus, when this voice declares, "You know me: lewd and lascivious/ la-la-la-lusty every minute of every day/ you know me getting la-la-la lucky/ it's the one thing the only thing only on my mind," there's really no way for the listener to approach what's piping into their ears except to relate it to desire itself, to Bob (in *Jack the Modernist*) writing that "desire is not satisfied; it's expelled." Behead the Prophet's frenzied chaos is the aural equivalent of that expulsion, what can be categorized as the multifarious orgasm, the syncopic moment rooted not only in the pleasures of skin, but in the harrowing deprivations and oft-concealed sensualities of history and its memories. That the thrust of the multifarious orgasm derives an aspect of its motion from resistance to normativity should not be surprising, and the radicality of Behead the Prophet's queer torrent serves as one bit of evidence of such movement.

Pause. Here's an exercise: can you remember the first orgasm you experienced to music?

I knew nothing about Behead the Prophet when, at twelve years old, I picked up the group's CD at Repo Records in Bryn Mawr, Pennsylvania. I'd spent the previous two years dwelling in a truncated grief, as I'd not only come to the conclusion that I was queer, but also had a mother who had been crawling the shores of mortality with stage IV invasive epithelial cancer of the ovaries. Though she had emerged from her illness and was in remission, the impossibility of her ever truly recovering was laid bare by a newfound religiosity, which confronted my burgeoning sexuality in any number of predictable and unpredictable ways. As the cruel banality of the imagination would assume, my hints at my sexuality were treated as my obsession with punk and hardcore was treated: as part of an early teenage rebellious phase that would pass.

But in my bedroom, I was voracious. I read magazines like *Profane Existence* and *The Defenestrator* and *HeartattaCk* from front to back, steeping my consciousness in the weird brew of DIY punk and radical politics. I listened to records over and over again, by groups like... well, Behead the Prophet, Capitalist Casualties, Submission Hold, and Kill the Man Who Questions. And as is typical for a thirteen-year-old, I masturbated with an astonishing frequency in a vast array of positions and situations.

Yet the first time I can remember the music that was playing when I achieved orgasm, the scene itself was rather staid, normal even. I was lying in bed nude, walls surrounding me covered in a claustrophobic density of posters, left index finger up my asshole, stroking furiously, and Behead the Prophet's "In the Garden" was playing on my CD boombox. And then! There it was: a splash on the "sun air moon and soil [...] in the garden of incendiaries," the lyrics positing my young queer body as an explosive device.

I didn't think much of the circumstances at the time, but in retrospect, that orgasm can help form a frame for the collision of New Narrative and queer punk beyond the facility of a shared fascination with (and occasional yen for) abjection.

You see, I'm still that queer punk kid. "I can't imagine a place for myself in the world," as Bob writes in his own story of recollected youth in "Do Be. Don't Be." But unlike Bob, I've never trusted the world enough to allow myself to think it could imagine a place for me. "To take revenge on the world for not existing" remains the goal, and this is perhaps where that orgasm comes in again: not only to take revenge, but also to proclaim: "we're the freaks in town [...] [and we're] not down with this normal world junk."

III.

In 2011, I was asked to give a talk at Small Press Traffic, and after the usual search for a subject, I settled on what can be handily described as an anti-capitalist rant about the coffee-table book *Punk House: Interiors in Anarchy*. Though rife with the sort of talkiness, bluster, and oversharing that was more in vogue during that period, while reading through the talk again, I stumbled upon the following sentences, where I describe my headspace during a sexual encounter:

> What I'm really pondering [...] is how the sound of my head hitting the [shower stall] wall reverberates, and how shoddy the construction of the hotel must be. In a way, I am thinking about money, but more about its tactile failures than the rewards it can yield me.

And then, as if being sent back to that shower stall in SoMa wasn't enough, the next paragraph throws down the gloves:

Recognizing these failures [of capital] is part of what being a punk is all about. Of course, it's also what being a critical thinker and present in our world is all about, but the difference I've found is that most punks I know act on this recognition in their everyday lives. They don't just blather about it or blog about it or write about it in some book only other book-writers will read—they make an effort to subvert capital in the places they move through, the spaces they inhabit.

My naivete is showing to a certain degree, yes, and the whole mess seems quaintly bygone given the events that have taken place in Oakland during the past six years, but the multifarious orgasm is there: a postcard sharing intimacies from a once and future queer dissident.

When I wrote the talk, I lived in a queer punk house with a rotating cast of residents. At one point, there were five queer cis-gender weirdo dudes and a genderfluid Australian overstaying their visa living in a one-floor, four-bedroom dump. It was impossibly cheap and also impossible: the air was heavy not just with the particulate matter endemic to West Oakland, but also the stench of strange food and sex and beer and cigarettes and frying electricity and old plumbing. The Australian told my future partner that listening to us fuck made them wet, but that it might be a good idea to invest in a ball-gag. Too intimate, let's venture to say.

But that period remains instructive: we were a bunch of queer punks approaching our 30s, working shit jobs to eat and make rent but otherwise dwelling in a space against time, a luxurious world of good kinky sex and bicycling to the beach and flashing the middle finger to the loft-dwellers that were then really starting to stake a foreboding foothold in West Oakland. We woke up "excluded from the day ahead," as Bob would have it, but not altogether unhappy with that fate.

When Dodie writes about laughing at hegemony, at "the suggestion that freedom equals consumption equals human value," her laughter was ours—we existed in an unceasing chuckle sometimes raised to a manic braying. At the time, it seemed the most appropriate response to the unwavering brutality of the diurnal, to the conditions kari writes toward almost smack in the middle of *Bharat jiva*:

> waking up after waking up
> after another artificial anti-depressive smile
> wakes up individually wrapped cheese
> freezing not unlike a lisp
> stammering and stuttering to stay warm
> uncountried, constantly under flag
> freezing trying to wake up
> flanked by
> freezing heads in cars
> bodies in malls

Our laughter's analog is in that stammer, the attempt "to stay warm" in the "individually wrapped / ignored historical doritos nacho cheese / cool ranch next to/ doritos reduced fat nacho cheesier." Over time, most of us who lived in that house found our cackles turning to stammers as the conditions changed, the situations we found ourselves in becoming ever more dire, our alienation under late capital blooming as the apocalypse, the bland dread of "the natural white nacho/ cheese." Though the remainder of the lyrics are inscrutable, the chorus of Behead the Prophet's "Separated States" is just that two-word phrase yelled desperately over and over again, and its succinct evocation of "individually wrapped" despair is as much a balm as kari's poems—evidence that in our queerness, in our horror and estrangement from each other, there are others like us damning the same strictures even as they attempt to engulf us.

IV.

Much has been made of New Narrative's somewhat recent emergence from a decades-long concealment in the foggy streets of San Francisco, yet given the continued obscurity of some of its most prominent works and adherents, its reputation as an "underground literature" remains intact, despite where we're sitting. For example, when I mentioned New Narrative in passing in an article I recently wrote for a Philadelphia-based literary magazine, my editor asked me to expand upon what New Narrative is, for while she had a general idea, most readers—even those with erudite and eclectic tastes—do not.

And while academic studies have been published about queer punk aesthetics, most bands have yet to cross over into mainstream, or even subcultural, consciousness. For every Hunx & His Punx or Pansy Division, there is a group like Livid or Myles of Destruction. What I am getting at is that both New Narrative and queer punk work on various levels of the liminal, hovering between zones of recognition and obscurity. When Bob gives one of his rare readings or queercore powerhouse Limp Wrist perform a rare San Francisco show, the venues are packed, albeit the former is crowded with literary connoisseurs both queer and straight, and the latter is crowded with a mob of sweaty, slamdancing queer punks yelling along to lyrics like, "I love hardcore boys / I love boys hardcore." These two crowds might rub shoulders or more in the pissoir of the Eagle, but otherwise, their shared status of belonging to an "underground" scene is often tenuous at best.

Still, there is "night, and they walk unsane, sprawling chins of steel, / the fearless, the torn, the lamentable... / freaks of the underworld," as Kevin has written. I remember sharing a copy of *Jack the Modernist* with my queer housemates, and after each reader, the book was more and more sticky. We'd go to punk shows in basements together and make jokes about prolapse and glory holes and unattractive dudes jerking off to us at the bathhouse, but these friends seemed totally uninterested in accompanying me to hear Bruce read from the re-issued *The Truth About Ted*. The literary world of San Francisco was outside of the interstitial zone of the pissoir, and thus outside of comfort for these queer comrades, and the possibility of *living* in the pissoir and occupying both the liminal spaces of punk and New Narrative seemed outlandish to them in a way I couldn't understand. A good friend, who wrote gorgeous zines about his queerness and sex work, would sometimes respond to my praise with a series of questions: "But who cares about this other than me, you, and a few of our friends? Why write for anyone?" I told him that he sounded like Phyllis from *Jack* when she questions Bob, "Why should I *want* to be a writer?"

These are valid questions, and it seems that both Phyllis and my friend were understandably ambivalent about the idea of the writerly identity, the sort of enclosure that can create. But I've always respected the writerly identity as a sort of commons, a space to "explore the meeting of flesh and culture, the self as collaboration." What about the "enjambments of power, family, history, and language" made them uncomfortable with claiming an identity that they belonged to and belonged to them as much as it belonged to anyone, everyone? What lines had been fed to them that so scorched a boundary around the writerly identity that they could not cross?

Departing from Phyllis and focusing more on my friend, I think that what prevented him and many queer punks from entering the literary world at their fingertips was a sort of class anxiety. Many writers grouped around the New Narrative rubric have become members of the petit bourgeoisie as time has passed—along with those who own multiple properties or are active as landlords, it is difficult to imagine any in the New Narrative coterie who do not perform some of the unpaid social labors of the class as identified by James C. Scott, such as creating or fostering "the aesthetic pleasures of an animated and interesting streetscape, a large variety of social experiences and personalized services, acquaintance networks, [and] informal neighborhood news and gossip."

Thus, while there are plenty of self-identified queer punks who come from middle-to-upper-middle class backgrounds, myself included, there are a great many who would be categorized as the proletariat, including those who have been kicked out of these more luxe backgrounds. Entering a world of small ownership, where personal and social autonomy is the great prize, is not some easy feat for many queer punks, in other words, and while many of those within the New Narrative milieu are theoretically radical, when it comes down to self-reflection coupled with actual class analysis, a number of the writers within the movement fail. I could tell some stories, but here I'm going to buck the New Narrative tendency toward public gossip and simply let the imagination ruminate.

V.

I'm going to end this talk, probably prematurely, with another admission: I'm embarrassed of my time spent with New Narrative. In her "Irresponsible Essay" course at CCA, Dodie's first assignment was to write the most embarrassing thing about yourself that you felt you could share, a common prompt within the New Narrative workshop scene. I wrote about the first time I came, watching *Full House* on a tiny analog screen, honed in on the bulge in John Stamos' pants. Later in that course, I wrote a piece about my granny's recent death, how I couldn't stop eyeing the altar boys at her funeral service. (They weren't children, get your mind out of the gutter). A year or so later, Kevin asked to publish a piece about technology and masturbating to cam porn in the *Best New Gay Erotica* that he was editing.

New Narrative and its devices liberated me, and that's embarrassing. That I needed liberating is embarrassing. That *my writing* needed liberating is embarrassing. But I did, and it did, and my writing is partly the fault of Dodie and Kevin and Camille and Bob and Bruce and Steve and Dennis and Rob and any number of other people, both dead and alive. Like punk rock and its collaborative spirit, New Narrative wends its way through so much of what I write and think and read towards, and I am simultaneously grateful and totally vexed by that dynamic.

Perhaps I feel hesitation and discomfort when acknowledging the perpetual effects that the fellow travelers of queer punk and New Narrative have on me, because both are outlandish, oft-controversial, and rarely stable. I've lived in seven different places in seven different towns in the past two years, I've helped alienate any number of people during that time, and I've often felt like a being from another planet during the process. A mirror held to my own failings is unsettling at best and scream-inducing at worst.

"There's something in my veins, and it's trying to fucking kill me." David Wojnarowicz was ostensibly yelling to an empty street about AIDS, but he was also yelling about the multifarious orgasm: the "enjambments of power, family, history, and language" which, along with syncopic pleasure, run through all of our veins, and are also actively trying to kill us. Where New Narrative burrows in and investigates, punk rock tells these strictures off. "Given the options, where would your anger take you? —where has it taken you?"

Dear Hole

Absence my presence is, strangeness my grace
—Fulke Greville, *Caelica (LXIX)*

Only Blue Talks

Bob, slurp
at day-glo indigos
of unsubtle neck
tightening in hand

a sort of folk
prelude to dew
approximates the fun
of prayers, yours

where harmony
venns with sharing
skull and a willow
framing mine

dysfluent there
at your t'weren't
unnecessary affair
at the equinox, yea

a termed needle
which transfixes
pointing to pools
and high platforms.

The Wonder of Wonder

Was it a garden or an illustration
depicts these screens reflecting
skin, eely though not unpleasant
and its perforations commingling
with grunts for *MORE CREAMER*

Was it a golden brown shag
or the fox tracking my eyes
pleading for simple port, that is
there should be a part for my kidneys
elsewhere but here's his gracilis

Was it a narrow hall or did I
feel him riding in haze
through the gulch, reverse, gulch
that I pour through damning the brick
brought me to this place in my birth

Generating and Arounding

As if he packed
my memory into
dankest swell look
at my spirit wagging
its ass on Turk
perpetual skinny
in threadbare
strings of saliva
hardened as nature
foams and squalid
portions bare hiss
of sun warping
cassette I remember
we sang some meat
market song unbuttoned
in elevator his lips
laughing in his twin
bed my fullest
range his name
and the fire escape.

Munch Munch Said

Kept swallowing
glitter, that skeleton
shadow raunch
festooned under
le moi, we knew
our stank bloomed
like insects violining
and to utmost right there, yes,
locale that loves punch
and I worked him
into a nimbus wiggling
in tight waitress slacks,
you felt that wink?

Walk Down the Street
Like a Motherfucker

One of my meats against
the wall, demands your palm
reach there and hold
the glass of soju in cold
sweet evening, I wept
to spite my drowning
tub I made for our skins
in my mind, I'm going
to burn *Utopias* then
wipe you incorrect pick
what you dried on mine
prominent cheekbone, see
you in jade morning slick
at mirror, that contour
rummaged pinks in me
I'd merely read of, thrown
onto the rug like happy baby
happy baby licked the tar,
pressed lit cig to crown
then gulped then called
a morpheme like I never
walked the same again.

Eluctable Recipe

A delight I've addressed
previously, shirt rolled
to my sternum's inelastic
density sparring braces
now winged on tile, gentle
like a cake he's thinking
toward and in quivering
arched back, allowing
to be baked in me much
in my character, wanting
heat and moving too close
like a caveman I need
to feel so often the sad
fact of ecstasy's diminishing
returns even as I scoop
my pinky then place it
on my tongues, as if
I were a violent man instead
of what's borne yet leaking
down my hocks.

You're Swank

I apologize in advance
for the soup's consistency
and mouthfeel, I loosen it
and shower later though
it was *his* face

The Condominium Development
Built on My Semen

The sort of sex
shop you wince at
going in, if even
to walk the stairs
with a camera
squeezing trigger
thigh back okay

Bleak palindrome
or the eastern light
leak in this rubber
room or series of
my throat wrapped
around and dripping
capturing it dripping

all loose like spray
thumb circling "bullock"
boy me with a cherry
in cheek the linger
I imagine being
consumed without
feeding but am lost

pulsing my hands
on his hips how
loose I may say
how loose
thus I plunged

enunciate articulate
or never speak

I know it's false
but please graft
here to ride please
here and tighten
his tit in my fist
fluorescent light
and then like water

The Chicken Place

Stern and sick
on the landing
goodbye, though
hair acrid follicle
taste the third
molar inhabited
with you, my absence
slips this way
as you puff
on my pouty boy
lips just attached
to my face like earlier,
finishing my eggs
easy as I exit
and enter and
grab the ashtray, repeat.

It's Big and It's Gold

It wasn't a date we were on
the guy's face recalled eggplant

parm oozing his cheeks, eyes
and ears and mouth and nose

I had forgotten yours but the club
was a cave, soiled in that way

leaning in soils so deftly, skin
daring my sense a running jump

off the bridge or at least suckle
jugular news from you, fingers

inside my shorts it gained.
Young in an old man's tent

your righteous need to smoke
after as I reassembled the leopard

down your hip and thigh, I never
could wait to rip it off and thus

how I knew your season, to speak
on the concourse of April

which is an attempt to fill
every cup and every face

I made for you, make for you
what you can't see, what your slug

pressing my rose causes
us, filaments in growing bulb.

Bill in My Mouth

If I were pig in pit, eyelid sweat thus
more possible but he removes himself
eyeing himself scenting one hand, yelling
he's just some punker, another index
finger stroked or resting you sullow
the moo of my resistance you might
have learned more about dummy chew
chew chew resembles the slap and pearls
of fluid dripping the fat grab, associate me
with that vein that emerges or some
scum gracing your marble

Gude Laune

Centered, that is in repetition
of my neck bowed to crease
into your visage somewhere
between deaths, aloft
and slightly dumb watching
me like the glove I am
thwacking your belly
at a Balearic beat, no sight
of land our song of praise.

Epilogue:
My Rectum, My Grave

I.

I knew I was dying in that hole. There was too much blood and mucus spurting. It either rained for days on end or served hard broiler. My fingers stained the filters with clay then loam as I kept digging.

A former lover wrote me, "I'm so into snuff, this is so hot," and I didn't know how to respond. I was dying in that hole. Yowled through the evening to find myself unable to sleep, ass sore and needing cool. In the photo, my shorts rode above where my cock begins and there's a slight cum gutter forming, abdominals peeking out an unbuttoned shirt.

Now this is where I wear a bag that catches my shit. It's attached with a combination of a paste and an adhesive flexible wax wafer with an opening big enough for my stoma. I was dying in that hole. There is no satisfaction in knowledge.

I miss wearing the shirt that I was wearing in the grave, now too tight to accommodate my shape. The niche or shelf is there to support the board placed over the body. What occurs to pleasure, to absence, to fullness when such a removal happens. I was dying in that hole.

II.

"This was the patient's first
colonoscopy which showed
Malignant partially obstructing
tumor in the rectum extending
almost to the anal verge.

Pathology adenocarcinoma.

CT scan revealed the known
tumor and several sub centimeter
mesorectal fascia nodes
an enhancing left distal external
iliac node suspicious for mets."

III.

I was dying in that hole. The absence is removed though an absence remains. On the phone I asked him whether he remembered the light turning the room an obscene curl of tangerine when he fucked me for the first time, his porn star dick slamming me as he held my legs aloft. In this procedure, a flexible narrow tube with a light and tiny camera on the end is utilized to explore.

Fullness is measured by absence, but as the absence is absent, fullness finds itself unable to reach itself. I was dying in that hole. The old man swirled his tongue in and out of my cheeks as I admired the original Hujar print on the facing wall. He told me to drop trou while we waited for his assistant to fetch the implement, and I obliged.

The issue then becomes one of pleasure's possibility in this state of truncated fullness. In a review of the scene entitled "Use The Stud's Uncut Cock As A Shot Glass At A Public Bar!" user *sportboy* writes "I hope you recruited the blond punk as a permanent actor?!" I was dying in that hole. They told me to get up on the table and to recline on my left side, then lift my right buttock with my hand.

In the unyielding permanence of this absence, it would be facile to assess that pleasure, too, has been truncated. His frame was sinewy yet compact, and he alternated his tempo as he spat on me and twisted my nipples so hard they bled. My surgeon lubricated the sigmoidoscope and inserted it with little effort, and I laughed and exclaimed, "Paint me like one of your French girls!" I was dying in that hole.

IV.

"Discussed with the patient that given his Lynch Dx, total proctocolectomy is indicated given the almost certain need for chemoradiation pre-op, and that anatomically an intersphincteric resection would be needed, I feel that reconstruction with a J-pouch would likely yield very poor functional results, and that abdominoperineal resection surgery would be recommended."

"An abdominoperineal resection (APR) is a surgery in which the anus, rectum, and sigmoid colon are removed. This procedure is most often used to treat rectal cancers located very low in the rectum."

V.

I was dying in that hole. My apologies for repeating myself, for exposing myself to you this way, but I cannot fathom another method of returning to my pleasure and my fullness except by explaining the absence that is my present, that which is most conspicuous every time I feel desire. Bersani famously argues that in the collective mind emerging and evidenced from thousands of years of social history, *"to be penetrated is to abdicate power."* So I ask: has my genetic and social tragedy forced me into a role where I am merely a tool of domination, or in other words: am I just another top?

My apologies for bringing theory into all of this, but I am so simultaneously uncomfortable with and repulsed and haunted by the loss of my absence that I spiral into the "anticommunal" narcissism of anxious self-talk. I was dying in that hole. The syncopic moment of being penetrated, where pleasure is measured by the keenest sense of what Bersani terms "self-abolition," feels like a scrapbook memory. What if my yearning is impossible because the physical center of my own abolition was carted off as medical waste in August 2019?

My apologies for dwelling in the lurid ramble that might be termed "my lost asshole," but I am desperate to relieve the psychic suffering that washes over me whenever I am physically aroused. That is, I am crying that I cannot even mistake my own "self-shattering as self-swelling," that I cannot tend to the ecstatic rupture that I remember. I was dying in that hole. If I cannot find a new way to delude myself or to abandon sense, what is the point of continuing?

My apologies for being melodramatic, but I am worried that the poverty of what fullness remains means that I will never again feel pleasure. My self is always in sight. Will I ever leave again? I was dying in that hole.

VI.

There is no satisfaction in any of this. I resisted turning this book into a trauma dumpster about family and illness, just as I resisted turning it into another stretch of recalling my slut years, and resisted transforming it into a systems composition that dully lists the hundreds of songs that played when they aimed radio-active lasers at my dick or the hundreds of side effects of the twenty-plus medications that I had to consume repeatedly over the course of eight months in 2019—nausea, "Proud Mary," nausea, diarrhea, nausea, diarrhea, cold neuropathy, "Surfin' USA," nausea, headache, "Burning Down the House," nausea, "Somewhere Over the Rainbow."

For the most part, my resistance failed. I was dying in that hole, but now I am living in it.

I need a new standard of care, I need to depart from the primacy of the anal, I need directions that might lead me to the sumptuousness of fusion, of looking at my love from above then embracing him beneath me, an "infinitely loved object of sacrifice," dissolve
dissolve
dissolve
dissolve
dissolve
dissolve
dissolve
dissolve
dissolve
dissolve
dissolve

dissolve

dissolve

dissolve

dissolve

dissolve

dissolve

dissolve

dissolve

dissolve

dissolve

dissolve

dissolve

dissolve

dissolve

dissolve

dissolve

dissolve

dissolve

dissolve

dissolve

dissolve

dissolve

dissolve

dissolve

dissolve

dissolve

dissolve

dissolve

dissolve

dissolve

dissolve

dissolve

dissolve

dissolve
dissolve
dissolve
dissolve
dissolve
dissolve
dissolve
dissolve
dissolve
dissolve
dissolve
dissolve
dissolve

dissolve

VII.

How does it mean, to yield to dissolution? Some would say that I have led a dissolute life, and they wouldn't be wrong. Before and since 2019, I've damaged myself both intentionally and unintentionally, acted foolish and prideful, picked fights, threatened my own bodily integrity, the list continues and continues. I have also tried to give myself over to love in the midst of my own private devastation and the devastation that surrounds us all.

But that is the *what*, not the *how*.

The *how* arrives with the obvious fact that if the chemistry and timing is right, any dissolution forms a solution. What I am trying to do—what I've tried to do—is form a solution, or many solutions, so that I might continue with my absence, to become a fullness in absence's knowledge, pleasures, and displeasures. That pleasure might be had, still, in knowledge, in displeasure. I am simply weary of dissolving any further.

VIII.

There is a short pornographic film clip that I have come to adore. Its action depicts two young men wearing tight white briefs while fighting over and spraying each other with a regular garden hose. They eventually press against one another, then move to a hammock, where they kiss and rub, one on top of the other. The camera moves between a shot of their semi-horizontal, swaying torsos flexing in a languorous rhythm and an overhead view of the buttocks of the twink on top, whose supple flesh is wet against the soaked white fabric of the briefs. Given his position, one can imagine how his ass would look without the briefs, his hole puckering and releasing in the open air. Then, the camera closes in on where the young men meet most intensely, and the viewer sees the dick of the twink on top peeking through his sodden underwear, pink and throbbing. The clip ends with the two reposing next to each other, the larger twink on his back and the more lithe one on his side, laying his head on his lover's chest.

The clip removes me from myself because it recalls my earliest memories of intimacy: resting my hand on my bandmate's inner thigh during the movie screening, reaching my hand down the front of a willing boy's jeans in our middle school's abandoned fallout shelter, making out with boys at summer camp and sneaking into each other's rooms to sleep next to each other because we didn't want to say goodnight, rubbing against another freshman in the mildewed basement of a co-op.

I am relating these moments to you because I have worried that returning to the sweetness of these acts places my living passion outside of the present. But as the clip I described moves in slow-motion, so has my realization that *it is this very sweetness that I desire most.*

I place my naked body on the naked body of another man, and I become full.

I place my naked body on the naked body of another man, and I lose myself.

I place my naked body on the naked body of another man, and I forgive my tragedy and return to myself, humming against him, saturated.

IX.

If I write that I did not expect the book to end this way, you might not believe me, but it would be the truth.

I am suspicious of the redemptive arcs of cancer survival narratives, partly because I do not believe in Sontag's bifurcated citizenship model of wellness and illness. There is no border between these states, and so pretending to one is merely another bad metaphor.

That is to say, despite appearances to the contrary, I will always be sick. I may be well enough to assume the position of a "well" person, but my sickness remains. It remains with all people who have been sick, as indelible in physical and emotional memory as laughter.

Nearly every day during my month-long stint of radiation therapy, I ended up driving behind a towed food cart that had a large, faded adhesive on it with an image of bottled water and the following words:

"WE USED BOTTLED WATER IN OUR SOUPS"

It became a sort of mantra for me, an elaboration of the unwell absurdity that was mine and the world's. I am sick, as sick as this world, and I love this lament, you in it, too.

Acknowledgments

Previous versions of some of the writing appeared in *Full Stop*, *Vestiges*, *The Brooklyn Rail*, and *Senna Hoy* (in both English and French, translated by Théo Robine-Langlois). Many thanks to the *Full Stop* crew, Jared Daniel Fagen, Anselm Berrigan, Luc Bénazet, and Jackqueline Frost for giving the pieces their first homes. Some readers will also recognize poems from fugitive chapbooks—many thanks to you wild ones.

Many thanks to Catriona Strang for allowing me to re-print the entirety of "www.sorry.com" in "Make Me Real, Make Me Sick." I only hope that its inclusion may serve as a testament to the power of Strang's work with Nancy Shaw, and as a suitable memorial to Shaw's astonishing life and writing.

"Taking Revenge on the World for Not Existing" was originally delivered as a talk at *Communal Presence: New Narrative Writing Today*, a conference held at UC-Berkeley from October 13-15, 2017. Parts of it have been altered for publication.

"Can't Get You Out of My Head" was written with the help of GPT-2, a predecessor to the now-ubiquitous ChatGPT. I was missing Kevin Killian, my departed mentor, and wanted to speak with him, and so began pasting our emails to each other into the LLM's prompt box. I arranged what emerged into what is in this book, which was originally published under the title, "Conversations With Kevin."

A few of these poems were written as part of workshops or alternative writing spaces. Many thanks to Sophia Dahlin and Violet Spurlock's 2021 August Cult for all of "Big Dearth in Whir," and thanks to those on the Tilden-Obeisanct Landing and PRB Discord for dealing with me ;-)

My dear friend Syd Staiti took a first look and gave marvelous feedback on an earlier draft of *Hand Me the Limits*. I am forever grateful for his kindness and camaraderie through the years.

Without the love of the following friends, I wouldn't be able to write poems at all: Ryan Skrabalak, Danielle LaFrance, Eric Sneathen, Mark Francis Johnson, Sarah DeGiorgis, Erin Morrill, Oki Sogumi, Adam Kaplan, Jason and Marta Mitchell, Levi Bentley, Zach Ozma, Julian Shendelman, Allison Chomet, Leo Famulari, Lucinda Trask, Joshua Castaño, Kyle Chvasta, Brittany Taylor, Ami Dang, Zach Christensen, Jasmine Gibson, John Rufo, Clint Burnham, Gordon Faylor, Syd Zolf, Julia Bloch, Christy Davids, Jenn DiGuglielmo, Laurence Jones, Nora Treatbaby, Joseph Mosconi, Anna Gurton-Wachter, Ian Dreiblatt, Helen Stuhr-Rommereim, Mike Schapira, Zan de Parry, and Chelsea Hogue, among too many others to name. I love you all with an immensity that is at times overwhelming.

Many thanks to Kay Gabriel, Cecily Nicholson, and Jean Day for spending time with this book. Your consideration means a great deal.

Finally, as ever, this book is for Theo, Canela, and Wiz, as well as my parents, Tom and Josephine. Because of you, I am lucky to be here.

Ted Rees is a poet, essayist, and editor living and working in Philadelphia. He is the author of *Dog Day Economy*, *Thanksgiving: a Poem*, and *In Brazen Fontanelle Aflame*.

His essays have been published in *The Back Room*, *The Poetry Project Newsletter*, *Libertines in the Ante-Room of Love: Poets on Punk*, *Full Stop Quarterly*, and *ON Contemporary Practice's monograph on New Narrative*. He is Associate Editor for The Elephants, as well as founder and co-editor of Asterion Projects with Levi Bentley.

ROOF BOOKS

the best in language since 1976

Recent & Selected Titles

- SECRET SOUNDS OF PONDS by David Rothenberg, 138 pp. $29.95
- THE POLITICS OF HOPE (After the War): Selected and New Poems by Dubravka Djuric, Biljana D. Obradovic (translator), 248 pp. $25
- BAINBRIDGE ISLAND NOTEBOOK by Uche Nduka, 148 pp. $20
- MAMMAL by Richard Loranger, 128 pp. $20
- EXCURSIVE by Elizabeth Robinson, 140 pp. $20
- I, BOOMBOX by Robert Glück, 194 pp. $20
- FOR TRAPPED THINGS by Brian Kim Stefans, 138 pp. $20
- TRUE ACCOUNT OF TALKING TO THE 7 IN SUNNYSIDE by Paolo Javier, 192 pp. $20
- THE NIGHT BEFORE THE DAY ON WHICH by Jean Day, 118 pp. $20
- MINE ECLOGUE by Jacob Kahn, 104 pp. $20
- SCISSORWORK by Uche Nduka, 150 pp. $20
- THIEF OF HEARTS by Maxwell Owen Clark, 116 pp. $20
- DOG DAY ECONOMY by Ted Rees, 138 pp. $20
- THE NERVE EPISTLE by Sarah Riggs, 110 pp. $20
- QUANUNDRUM: [i will be your many angled thing] by Edwin Torres, 128 pp. $20
- FETAL POSITION by Holly Melgard, 110 pp. $20
- DEATH & DISASTER SERIES by Lonely Christopher, 192 pp. $20
- THE COMBUSTION CYCLE by Will Alexander, 614 pp. $25
- URBAN POETRY FROM CHINA editors Huang Fan and James Sherry, translation editor Daniel Tay, 412 pp. $25
- BIONIC COMMUNALITY by Brenda Iijima, 150 pp. $20
- QUEENZENGLISH.MP3: POETRY: POETRY, PHILOSOPHY, PERFORMATIVITY edited by Kyoo Lee, 176 pp. $20
- UNSOLVED MYSTERIES by Marie Buck, 96 pp. $18.95

Roof Books are distributed by
SMALL PRESS DISTRIBUTION • spdbooks.org
Roof Books are published by Segue Foundation
300 Bowery #2 • New York, NY 10012
seguefoundation.com